CAT PALS

disc

Crabtree Publishing Company
www.crabtreebooks.com
1-800-387-7650

Published in Canada
Crabtree Publishing
616 Welland Avenue
St. Catharines, ON
L2M 5V6

Published in the United States
Crabtree Publishing
PMB 59051
350 Fifth Ave, 59th Floor
New York, NY 10118

Published in 2018 by CRABTREE PUBLISHING COMPANY.

First published in 2017 by Wayland
Copyright © Hodder and Stoughton, 2017

Author: Pat Jacobs

Editor: Elizabeth Brent

Project coordinator: Kathy Middleton

Editor: Petrice Custance

Cover and Interior Design: Dynamo

Proofreader: Wendy Scavuzzo

Prepress technician: Samara Parent

Print and production coordinator: Margaret Amy Salter

Photographs:
All images courtesy of iStock: p1 Tsekhmister; p2 Tomwang112, 5second, Joanna Zaleska; p3 GlobalP; p4 Eric Isselée, Elena Butinova; p5 Eric Isselée; p6 GlobalP, kipuxa, Axel Bueckert, cynoclub; p7 Lilun_Li, GlobalP, ewastudio, Kirill Vorobyev; p8 Pavel Hlystov, scigelova, Benjamin Simeneta, estevessabrina, Dixi_; p9 nevodka, Meinzahn, Eric Isselée, Erik Lam, chendongshan; p10 Ysbrand, Cosijn, parrus, Konstantin Aksenov, Mykola Velychko; p11 Axel Bueckert, eAlisa; p12 Yuriy Tuchkov, MW47, unclepodger; p13 Aly Tyler, Voren1, alexandco; p14 erjioLe, Aleksandr Ermolaev, GlobalP, detcreative; p15 Magone, aguirre_mar, gemenacom, Julián Rovagnati, anna1311, rvlsoft, Egor Shabanov, Nastco; p16 Dorottya_Mathe; p17 Okssi68, RalchevDesign, Goldfinch4ever, Ryerson Clark, alfonsmartin; p18 Bart_Kowski, Wavebreakmedia; p19 dny3d, Eric Isselée, MoosyElk, suemack, mashimara; p20 GlobalP; p21 Tony Campbell, oksun70, Maciej Maksymowicz; p22 cynoclub, adogslifephoto; p23 vvvita, Pavel Hlystov, gsermek; p24 Barna Tanko, Azaliya, Ikoimages; p25 cassinga, gurinaleksandr, absolutimages, Butsaya, mbolina; p26 GrishaL, Voren1, Leoba; p27 peplow, 2002lubava1981, GlobalP; p28 kmsh, Dixi_; p29 pwollinga; p32 MilanEXPO.Front cover : Dixi_; Back cover: fotostok_pdv

Printed in the USA/072017/CG20170524

Library and Archives Canada Cataloguing in Publication

Jacobs, Pat, author
       Cat pals / Pat Jacobs.

(Pet pals)
Includes index.
Issued in print and electronic formats.
ISBN 978-0-7787-3550-2 (hardcover).--
ISBN 978-0-7787-3562-5 (softcover).--
ISBN 978-1-4271-1944-5 (HTML)

       1. Cats--Juvenile literature. 2. Cats--Behavior--Juvenile
literature. I. Title.

SF445.7.J33 2017   j636.8   C2017-902513-9
                                                            C2017-902514-7

Library of Congress Cataloging-in-Publication Data

Names: Jacobs, Pat, author.
Title: Cat pals / Pat Jacobs.
Description: New York, New York : Crabtree Publishing, 2018. |
    Series: Pet pals | Audience: Age 7-10. | Audience: Grade K to 3.
    | Includes index.
Identifiers: LCCN 2017016735 (print) | LCCN 2017027432 (ebook) |
    ISBN 9781427119445 (Electronic HTML) |
    ISBN 9780778735502 (reinforced library binding) |
    ISBN 9780778735625 (pbk.)
Subjects: LCSH: Cats--Juvenile literature.
Classification: LCC SF445.7 (ebook) | LCC SF445.7 .J33 2018 (print)
    | DDC 636.8--dc23
LC record available at https://lccn.loc.gov/2017016735

CONTENTS

Your cat from head to tail   **4**

Cat breeds   **6**

Choosing your cat   **8**

Cozy kitty   **10**

Settling in   **12**

Catering for kitty   **14**

Day-to-day care   **16**

Health and safety   **18**

Cat behavior   **20**

Communication   **22**

Training   **24**

Fun and games   **26**

Cat quiz   **28**

Quiz answers   **30**

Learning more   **31**

Glossary & Index   **32**

YOUR CAT FROM HEAD TO TAIL

Cats have lived with humans since the Ancient Egyptians. Cats were first welcomed into homes to keep snakes away and protect grain stores from rats and mice. Cats are **predators**, so they need to eat meat. Their bodies have **evolved** into expert hunting machines.

Spine: Their flexible spine allows them to twist when they fall, and land on their feet.

Tail: The tail is used for balance and communication, and it also has scent **glands**. Two cats may curl their tails together to transfer their scents.

Back legs: Powerful back legs act like springs, allowing cats to jump up to nine times their height.

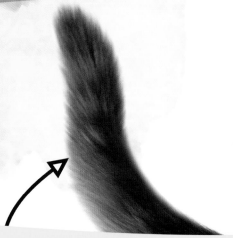

Claws: Claws are used for hunting, climbing, and self-defense. A cat's claws can **retract**, which allows it to silently sneak up on its **prey**.

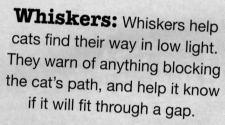

Ears: Each ear has about 30 muscles, which allow cats to move their ears in many directions. They can hear exactly where a sound comes from, and easily find their prey.

Eyes: Cats have a layer in their eyes that **reflects** light, so they can hunt in near-darkness. This is why cats' eyes glow at night.

Whiskers: Whiskers help cats find their way in low light. They warn of anything blocking the cat's path, and help it know if it will fit through a gap.

Tongue: A cat's tongue has tiny backward-facing spikes to scrape meat from bones, and also to help with grooming.

Nose: A cat's sense of smell is far stronger than ours. It has an extra pair of scent **organs** in the roof of its mouth.

Shoulders: Their tiny collarbones are attached to the shoulder blades by muscle, not bone. This allows cats to squeeze through spaces no larger than their head.

CAT FACTS

• If a cat curls its lips and opens its mouth, it is using its scent organs to get information about an interesting smell.

• Pet cats usually live for about 15 years, but an American cat, named Creme Puff, died just after her 38th birthday!

CAT BREEDS

There are more than 60 recognized **breeds** of cat, but most pet cats are a mix of breeds and come in all colors, shapes, and sizes.

Siamese cats are affectionate and talkative – they are well-known for their loud yowls. They are intelligent, inquisitive, and playful, so they do not like being left alone for long periods.

Bengal cats can leap to surprising heights, often performing somersaults in the air. They are noisy and energetic, and love to play with water.

Sphynx cats look hairless, but most have a fine layer of hair. Their skin has colors and markings like fur would have. They are friendly, intelligent, and curious, and known for their dog-like behavior.

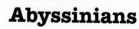

Abyssinians are very intelligent and inquisitive, with playful personalities. They enjoy going outdoors, are very active, and enjoy the company of another cat.

Birmans have deep blue eyes, silky fur, and white "gloves" on each paw. They enjoy company, so they don't like to be home alone. These quiet and curious cats will happily live with other pets.

Maine Coons are long-haired cats. They are excellent at hunting mice, and they have furry paws that allow them to walk on snow. These gentle giants get along well with other cats and dogs.

American Bobtail cats were bred from one American kitten with a very short tail. These fun-loving cats are great at escaping from places, and they love to travel and explore.

Devon Rex cats have a curly coat and large ears. These mischievous cats love to climb. They are quick to learn tricks, and they enjoy playing fetch with other cats and dogs.

CHOOSING YOUR CAT

A cat can be part of your family for many years! So before you fall in love with a cute kitten, it's a good idea to decide which type of cat will best fit into your household.

PEDIGREE OR MIXED?

Pedigree cats are more expensive than **mixed breeds**, and should always be purchased from a recommended **breeder**. There are often more mixed-breed cats available, and many can be found for adoption at your local shelter.

KITTEN OR ADULT CAT?

Kittens need a lot of attention at first. Someone will need to be at home all day to keep an eye on them. Adult cats are more independent, but even older cats need time and attention to help them settle in.

 LONG-HAIRED **OR** SHORT-HAIRED?

Long-haired cats shed hairs and need brushing every day. If you don't have time to brush them, a short-haired cat may be the best choice for you. Less grooming means more time for play!

MALE **OR** FEMALE?

Male cats are slightly bigger than females, but if they are **neutered** there is little difference between them. If you are buying a kitten, keep in mind that it is more expensive to **spay** a female cat.

 INDOOR CAT **OR** OUTDOOR CAT

Most cats are natural explorers, but many cities have rules about keeping cats indoors. House cats need a lot of attention so they don't become bored.

COZY KITTY

Before you collect your new kitten or cat, you'll need some equipment to help make your furry friend feel at home.

MEALTIME MUST-HAVES

Cats can be picky eaters, so buy a small selection of different foods to see which your cat prefers. Ceramic or stainless-steel bowls are best because some cats dislike the smell of plastic. Cats prefer wide, shallow bowls, so their whiskers don't brush against the sides.

PET CHECK ✓

Does your cat have:

- a litter box in a quiet part of your home?
- food and water bowls?
- somewhere to scratch?

PET TALK

I might feel nervous when I first move in, so please give me somewhere quiet to hide while I get to know my new home.

A reflecting collar will help drivers spot your cat if it gets out at night. A collar should stretch, so if it gets caught on something your cat can safely slide out of it.

A strong and secure carrier with plenty of air holes is the safest way to bring your pet home. The carrier can also be used for future trips to the vet.

You'll need a litter box and a good supply of cat litter, along with a poop-scooper to keep it clean. Place the box away from your cat's eating and sleeping areas.

Cats scratch to mark their **territory** and keep their claws sharp, so a scratching post may save your furniture!

Even short-haired cats need weekly grooming, so a grooming brush is an essential piece of a cat-care kit.

SETTLING IN

Bringing your cat home is very exciting, but it can be a little scary for your new friend. Prepare one warm, quiet room with food and water, a litter box, and somewhere cozy to sleep, so your cat can feel safe while it gets used to its surroundings.

ON ARRIVAL

When you get home, take the cat carrier into the prepared room and open it, leaving your pet alone to explore its territory. Cats like to hide when they go somewhere new. A cardboard box makes a great hiding spot!

MAKING FRIENDS

After a few hours, go into the room and sit quietly on the floor. You could take some toys and treats with you. Don't force your kitten to come to you or try to pick it up. If it is shy, it may take a few days before it feels confident enough to approach you.

STARTING TO EXPLORE

Your cat will let you know when it feels ready to explore the rest of your home by trying to follow you out of the room. Make sure all doors and windows leading outside are shut, and keep the door to the cat's room open so it can escape there if it gets scared.

GOING OUTSIDE

Cats should be kept indoors for two weeks after their arrival to make sure they don't get lost. Let your cat out for a few minutes just before a meal, then stand at the door with some food to encourage it back inside.

MEETING OTHER PETS

Cats and dogs communicate using smell, so exchanging bedding between pets is a good way to get them used to one another before they meet. Keeping one animal in a crate or behind a pet barrier allows you to introduce them without risk of harm. Don't leave two pets alone together until you are certain they have become friends.

13

CATERING FOR KITTY

Cats are **carnivores** and need to eat meat. Unlike dogs, they cannot survive on a **vegetarian** diet. Cats like to eat little bits often, so only feed them small amounts at a time instead of leaving food out all day.

FEEDING KITTENS

Kittens grow fast, so they need more food than adult cats. Kittens can start eating small amounts of kitten food at about four weeks old, and they should be fully **weaned** by the age of eight weeks.

FEEDING CATS

The easiest way to make sure your cat is getting all the **nutrients** it needs is to buy a good-quality cat food. Many cats prefer wet food, but they don't like it cold, so keep unopened packages or tins at room temperature.

Dry food is useful if you have to leave it out during the day.

PET TALK

Please do not feed me human foods such as chocolate, onions, and garlic, because they could make me sick.

DRINKING

Although cats don't drink much, fresh water should be available at all times, especially if your pet is eating dry food.

WEIGHT WATCHING

Pet cats have a regular supply of food and like to sleep a lot, so they can easily become overweight. A fat cat can suffer serious health problems, so be sure to limit the amount of treats it gets.

Milk is not suitable for cats. It can cause stomach upsets.

WEIGHT ☑ CHECK

- You should be able to feel your cat's bones beneath a thin layer of fat.
- Your cat should have a narrower waist behind the ribs when you look at it from above and from the side.

15

DAY-TO-DAY CARE

Check your pet for any sign of illness or injury every day. If your cat seems to be in pain or has stopped eating, it's time to visit the vet. It's much better to deal with any problems quickly so your furry friend doesn't suffer unnecessarily.

GROOMING

Brush your cat regularly – especially if it has long hair. This gets rid of loose hairs, which cats may swallow. It's also a good opportunity to check your pet for injuries. If cats swallow a lot of fur, hairballs form in their stomach and the cat will vomit them up.

I don't make a fuss if I feel sick, so it's important for my owner to notice any changes in my behavior.

FLEAS

Cat fleas are very common. They are tiny, but you might spot them when you are grooming your cat. There are many products to keep your pet flea-free, but some may make your cat sick. Ask your veterinarian which flea-prevention products are best for your pet.

WORMS

Cats can pick up worms from other animals, often from eating infected prey or from fleas. They often don't show any sign of having worms unless it becomes serious, so it's best to ask your vet about treatments to prevent worms.

TOOTH CARE

Taking care of your cat's teeth is a top priority. Cat toothpaste comes in fish or meat flavors, so start by letting your cat taste a little, then just touch its teeth with a cat toothbrush. As your pet gets used to the idea, start brushing its teeth gently.

HEALTH AND SAFETY

You can help make sure your pet stays safe and healthy by making sure medicines and household cleaners are stored out of reach, keeping windows and doors closed, and scheduling yearly visits to the vet.

VACCINATIONS

All kittens should be **vaccinated** against common cat diseases, and they will need regular vaccines as they grow. When you get a new cat, be sure to check which vaccinations it has had and when the next ones are due.

NEUTER/SPAY

Kittens are spayed or neutered when they are about four months old. It helps protect cats against some diseases. It also makes a happier homelife with your pet. A female cat can give birth to up to 200 kittens in her lifetime, and unneutered males tend to get into fights and spray urine to mark their territory.

I don't like going to the vet, but you can make it less scary for me by putting some of my bedding in the carrier so it smells like home.

MICROCHIPS

A microchip is the size of a grain of rice and is inserted under the cat's skin by a vet. If a lost cat is found, the microchip can be read and matched to the owner's contact details so they can be reunited.

POISONS

If you think your cat has been poisoned, take it to the vet at once. Cats may eat poisoned prey, such as mice, and some plants are dangerous for cats, especially those in the lily family. Cats may not swallow harmful substances on purpose, but could lick them off their fur.

TRAFFIC ACCIDENTS

You can reduce the risk of your cat getting hurt by a car by keeping it inside, especially at night. If your cat does go outside in the day, be sure to feed your cat early in the evening, so it is inside before dark.

PET CHECK ✓

Has your cat been:

- neutered or spayed?
- vaccinated?
- microchipped?

CAT BEHAVIOR

Cats hunt alone in the wild, and each cat needs an area large enough to provide enough to eat. Most male cats live on their own, but females and kittens may live in groups if there's plenty of food to go around. Pet cats are usually happy living alone, but some enjoy the company of other cats, especially if they have grown up together.

HIGH SPOTS

Cats like to observe their surroundings from a high place, so they can search for prey and watch out for danger. Many cats like to sit on a raised perch at home. too. Iif you have more than one cat, the leader will usually have the highest spot.

CATNAP

Cats sleep about 16 hours a day! They are most likely to be wide awake early in the morning and in the evening, when their prey would be most active if they were living in the wild.

PET TALK

I am most active in the early mornings and in the evening. That's the best time to play with me!

SCRATCHING

This is part of a cat's natural behavior. Cats have scent glands between their toes and it's one of the ways they mark their territory. Encourage your pet to use a scratching post by rubbing it with catnip and sprinkling some treats around the base.

HUNTING

Your cat has the **instinct** to hunt prey, even when it has plenty of food. You can help to satisfy this instinct by playing "cat and mouse" games with your pet, but don't be surprised if you still get a present of a dead mouse or bird!

COMMUNICATION

Knowing how cats talk to each other will help you understand what your pet is trying to tell you. Cats don't only communicate using sound—body language and scent are equally important to them.

BODY TALK

A cat's tail and ears are good clues to its mood. If its tail is straight up in the air and its ears are perky, the cat is feeling friendly. But if its tail is swishing from side to side and its ears are back, watch out! This is a warning that the cat is annoyed and may attack.

EYE CONTACT

When two cats meet they may challenge one another by staring, so your cat might not enjoy being stared at. A relaxed cat will blink or wink, and when your cat squints at you, that's the **feline** equivalent of a smile.

SUPER SNIFFERS

Cats have a great sense of smell. They use the scent glands on their faces, tails, and in between their toes to communicate. When a cat rubs its face on something or someone, it's marking its home turf and the members of its family group.

CAT CHAT

Cats chirp and meow as a greeting or to tell you it's time to get up and feed them. When cats get angry, they will hiss, snarl, and growl. Cats purr when they are happy and relaxed. Sick or injured cats may also purr to comfort themselves and help themselves get better.

TRAINING

The best way to train your cat is with a clicker and treats. First, get your cat to understand the connection between the sound of the clicker and a reward. When your cat obeys a command, press the clicker and then give it a tasty treat. You can teach your cat quite a few tricks this way!

CLICKER

CHECKING IN

Getting your cat to come when called is useful if your pet goes outside, and could save it from danger. Begin by calling your cat's name from one room and then pressing the clicker. Give your pet a treat as soon as it comes to you. When your cat understands, try calling it from a different room or from outside, and then click and reward.

PET TALK

Treats help me learn! If you give me a treat when I obey a new command, then I know I've done something to please you.

LITTER BOX

Take your kitten to its litter box when it wakes up and after every meal, then give it a click and a reward for using the box. Always keep the box in the same place and clean it out regularly. Don't use disinfectant or chemicals to clean the litter box as they may harm your cat.

MAKE A CAT RATTLE

Cats are sensitive to noise, so if your pet is scratching the furniture or jumping on the dining table, a sharp noise will send a message that this is not acceptable. Make a noisy cat rattle to discourage unwanted behavior by putting some pebbles in a tin with a lid.

HIGH FIVE

Hold up your hand with a treat wedged between two fingers. When your pet puts its paw up to get the treat, press the clicker and give it a reward. After you have practiced this, try the trick without the treat.

FUN AND GAMES

Cats love to play. It keeps them fit and alert and it's fun for their owners, too! Cats like toys that move so they can practice their hunting skills. There's no need to spend a lot of money, though. It's easy to make your own cat toys.

Cats are very curious and enjoy climbing and hiding, so a few cardboard boxes with entry and exit holes will keep them entertained for hours.

Throw a lightweight ball up the stairs so your cat can run after it as it rolls down.

Make a fishing-pole toy by tying feathers or tissue paper to some string or a stick, and wave it close to your cat.

CATNIP CRAZY

Catnip is a herb that many adult cats love. They will sniff it, lick it, rub against it, and roll in it. Try growing some in a pot or buy a cheap toy filled with dried catnip. Then sit back and enjoy watching your cat have some crazy fun!

Cats love chasing things. Try stuffing an old sock inside another and tying it to string. Drag it along in front of your cat using slow pulls and sharp jerks.

Blow some bubbles for your cat to chase.

TOP TIPS!

- Play for a short time every day
- Let your cat catch the toy at the end of each game
- Rotate toys so your cat doesn't get bored
- Put away toys after play to avoid accidents

CAT QUIZ

By now, you should know a lot about cats!

Test your knowledge by answering these questions:

1 How long does the average cat live?

a. 5 years
b. 15 years
c. 30 years

2 How many muscles do cats have in each ear?

a. 1
b. 10
c. 30

3 What is unusual about a Sphynx cat?

a. It is almost hairless
b. It has a curly coat
c. It has a short tail

4 How many hours does a cat sleep each day?

a. 8
b. 16
c. 20

5 Can a cat be a vegetarian?

a. Yes
b. Partly
c. No

6 Which plant makes some cats go crazy?

a. Catnip
b. Parsley
c. Mint

10 Which of these foods is harmful to cats?

a. Chocolate
b. Onions
c. Both

7 How is a cat feeling if its tail is swishing and its ears are back?

a. Happy
b. Relaxed
c. Angry

8 How many kittens will an average cat have during her life if she is not spayed?

a. 50
b. 200
c. 600

9 How often should you groom a short-haired cat?

a. Every day
b. Every week
c. Every month

QUIZ ANSWERS

1 How long does the average cat live?

b. 15 years

2 How many muscles do cats have in each ear?

c. 30

3 What is unusual about a Sphynx cat?

a. It is almost hairless

4 How many hours does a cat sleep each day?

b. 16

5 Can a cat be a vegetarian?

c. No

6 Which plant makes some cats go crazy?

a. Catnip

7 How is a cat feeling if its tail is swishing and its ears are back?

c. Angry

8 How many kittens will an average cat have during her life if she is not spayed?

b. 200

9 How often should you groom a short-haired cat?

b. Every week

10 Which of these foods is harmful to cats?

c. Both

LEARNING MORE

BOOKS

Bishop, Amanda, and Bobbie Kalman. *What is a Cat?* Crabtree Publishing, 2003.

Newman, Aline Alexander. *How to Speak Cat: A Guide to Decoding Cat Language.* National Geographic Children's Books, 2015.

Walker, Niki, and Bobbie Kalman. *Kittens.* Crabtree Publishing, 2004.

WEBSITES

http://pbskids.org/itsmylife/family/pets/article7.html
Check out this site for fun pet facts and great tips on caring for your pet pal.

http://kids.cfa.org/index.html
This site is all about cats! You'll find games, puzzles, coloring pages, and lots of interesting cat tips and facts.

www.lovethatpet.com/cats/
This website is full of helpful information about cat care. It even has funny cat pictures that will make you laugh out loud!

GLOSSARY

breed A group of animals with the same ancestors and characteristics

breeder A person who raises particular breeds of animals

carnivore An animal that mainly eats meat

evolve To slowly develop or change over generations

feline Another word for cat or cat-like

gland An organ that makes fluids and chemicals, such as saliva, tears, and scent

instinct Natural behavior that is automatic and not learned

mixed-breed A cat that has parents from at least two different breeds

neuter An operation that stops male animals from being able to make babies

nutrients The healthy elements of food, including protein, vitamins, and minerals

organ A part of a person, plant, or animal that performs a special function

pedigree An animal that has two parents of the same breed

predator An animal that hunts and eats other creatures

prey An animal that is hunted by other animals

reflect To throw back light or sound

retract To pull in

spay An operation that stops female animals from being able to have babies

territory An area an animal has claimed for itself and defends against intruders

vaccinate To inject with substances that protect animals and humans from serious diseases

vegetarian A type of diet that does not include meat or fish

wean When a baby is ready for solid food and no longer needs only its mother's milk

INDEX

Abyssinian cats 6
American Bobtail cats 7

Behavior 20, 21, 22, 23
Bengal cats 6
Birman cats 7
Breeds 6–7, 31

Catnip 21, 27
Claws 4, 11
Clickers 24
Collars 11
Communication 22–23

Devon Rex cats 7
Diet 14–15
Drinking 15

Ears 5, 22
Eyes 5, 22

Feeding 10, 14–15
Fleas 17

Games 21, 26–27
Grooming 9, 11, 16

Health 15, 16, 17, 18–19
Hunting 4, 20, 21, 26

Kittens 8, 9, 14, 18, 25

Litter box 11, 12, 25
Long-haired cats 9, 16

Maine Coon cats 7
Microchipping 19, 31
Mixed-breed cats 8, 31

Neutering 9, 18, 31
Noses 5

Pedigree cats 6–7, 8, 31
Playing 21, 26–27
Purring 23

Safety 13, 18–19
Scent 4, 5, 13, 21, 22, 23
Scent-marking 21, 23
Scratching 11, 21, 25
Short-haired cats 9, 11
Siamese cats 6

Sleeping 21
Spaying 8, 18
Sphynx cats 6

Tails 4, 22
Teeth 17
Tongues 5
Toys 26–27
Training 24–25

Vaccinations 18, 31

Weight 15
Whiskers 5, 10
Worms 17